Seership And The Spiritual

Evolution Of Man

Swami Bhakta Vishita

Kessinger Publishing's Rare Reprints

Thousands of Scarce and Hard-to-Find Books on These and other Subjects!

- Americana
- Ancient Mysteries
- Animals
- Anthropology
- Architecture
- Arts
- Astrology
- Bibliographies
- Biographies & Memoirs
- Body, Mind & Spirit
- Business & Investing
- Children & Young Adult
- Collectibles
- Comparative Religions
- Crafts & Hobbies
- Earth Sciences
- Education
- Ephemera
- Fiction
- Folklore
- Geography
- Health & Diet
- History
- Hobbies & Leisure
- Humor
- Illustrated Books
- Language & Culture
- Law
- Life Sciences

- Literature
- Medicine & Pharmacy
- Metaphysical
- Music
- Mystery & Crime
- Mythology
- Natural History
- Outdoor & Nature
- Philosophy
- Poetry
- Political Science
- Science
- Psychiatry & Psychology
- Reference
- Religion & Spiritualism
- Rhetoric
- Sacred Books
- Science Fiction
- Science & Technology
- Self-Help
- Social Sciences
- Symbolism
- Theatre & Drama
- Theology
- Travel & Explorations
- War & Military
- Women
- Yoga
- *Plus Much More!*

We kindly invite you to view our catalog list at:
http://www.kessinger.net

LESSON XIV

SPIRITUAL EVOLUTION OF MAN

You have learned from the previous chapter that man in his present state has a physical body, an etheric body, an astral body, and an ego. The ego is the controlling force, and works from within. There is the sentient soul, the intellectual soul and the self-conscious soul, of the lower level; and a spirit-self, the life-spirit and the spirit man, of the higher level. The relations between these are very closely interwoven with the whole universe. By studying these we gain a deeper insight into the mysteries of man's being.

In a later chapter you will be shown how to develop your latent faculties for looking backward, by means of perception. The primeval past has left its records. Once a being comes into existence, his spiritual forces never perish. They leave behind them their traces; their exact copies, in the spiritual foundations of the world. A seer, by using his perceptive faculty, can see through the visible to the invisible world, and attain a vast spiritual view, which is somewhat like a panorama, in which is recorded all the past events of the world's history.

The supersensible spheres, of course, cannot be investigated without the aid of spiritual perception, but when investigated by a seer they can be understood by the ordinary powers of thought. In the following pages the various conditions of the earth's evolution will be given, as seen by a seer. If you will study closely you will see that what you know at present has been evolved from the far distant past; and you will say, "Seership is logical—it proves how everything can be understood.

GLIMPSE OF THE HIGHER WORLDS

At the present time man lives in three states—the waking state, the sleeping state, and a state between the two—a dream state. This latter state we have already taken up, but it will be discussed again later. For the present, we will only concern ourselves with waking and sleeping.

Knowledge of the higher worlds is obtained by man when, in addition to the sleeping and waking, he attains to yet a third soul-state. While awake, the soul is given up to the impressions of the senses. While asleep, the sense impressions are latent, but the soul itself loses its consciousness, and whatever has happened during the day is gulfed into an ocean of unconsciousness.

The soul, for instance, might become conscious during sleep, even if sense-impressions were absent. We apparently have no memory of what has happened during the day, but would this be the same with the soul? Could it not have experiences? As the soul is capable of experiencing anything, even though we have no conscious recollection of it, then would that soul be asleep, so far as the external world is concerned, but it would be awake to the actual world.

This state of consciousness can be understood by following the advice as to the development of Seership. Everything the soul may communicate about those worlds which transcend the senses, has been discovered under similar conditions of consciousness. The means by which the conditions of consciousness are discovered will here be given.

In only one way does this consciousness resemble sleep. That is, that all outward activity of the senses ceases, and all thoughts, such as might be aroused by the action of the senses, stop. But it is different than in ordinary sleep, as then the soul is without the power required for conscious experience; it is just this power that this state of consciousness is to place in its control. From this power the soul is given the capacity to understand and be alive to such experiences as, under ordinary conditions of life, can be brought only by the action of the senses. The awakening of the soul to this higher consciousness is one of the states of Seership.

Seership leads one away from the ordinary consciousness into a condition of the soul during which the organs of spiritual perception are developed. These lie latent in each soul, and only need cultivation to bring forth results. When this development takes place, the person will become conscious of a change affecting his entire being. His experience with the material world will never have so affected or taken possession of him, or been so satisfying to him, nor have suffused him with such a sense of inner warmth, as does the experience to which he has now obtained access, invisible though it be to the physical eye, and not sensed by the physical touch. There is nothing so strengthening as to know and feel life's security.

You are now ready to take up the training which will develop Seership. This I want you to understand is not a special gift to a few. Every one has the rudimentary organs of the soul which can be developed for higher perception. Those who do not feel that they are ready to develop Seership, and are not especially impelled toward doing something for their own development, must remember that they stand under the guidance of spiritual powers, and that, when these unite, they are ready. Those powers will reveal to the soul, another world.

Some are of the opinion that it is wrong to interfere with the wisdom of such spiritual guidance. For those who think this way, a physical example is needed to show them that they are wrong. I will say, for instance, a man has a fine horse, but it has never been broken to harness; therefore, it is of no practical use to the owner at the present time. You are the same way. If you have been given organs for development, but have let them be idle, they are of no use. When you were given the rudiments of those organs necessary for the higher state of consciousness, they were intended to be developed. It is your duty to do all you can to develop them. This development of the inner faculties of the soul means a direct invasion of man's most-hidden sanctuary. It involves a certain change of the entire human being; the means of such a change cannot be evolved by any ordinary procedure of thought, for the knowledge of the manner in which such higher worlds are attained is possible only to those to whom the road is opened by experience. Every one has the right to influence the innermost sanctuary of his soul. Heretofore, it was not considered wise to set down in book form rules for developing the organs of spiritual perception, but I have come to the conclusion that no harm can be done. The time is here when the truths relating to the spiritual world should be made known. Human evolution has evolved the state when many persons are ready for the whole truth.

I will now take up a definite plan of training. There are many paths that reach the same goal, but from experience I think that the one I have adopted for this work is the most satisfactory. It always keeps you in control of your consciousness. It would be all right for you to lose your consciousness at times, if you were controlled by a thoroughly conscientious and highly developed teacher. Unfortunately, however, there are not many of these, so I would advise that you keep control of your consciousness.

You can gain the higher state of consciousness, only by proceeding from the ordinary waking-day consciousness. This is the consciousness that the soul experiences prior to its uplifting. Training, as outlined by us, will lead to a transcending of such consciousness. First, you will be instructed how to control yourself during the waking consciousness. The most apparently significant acts are very important. The soul must be occupied with only certain conceptions, which have a wonderful influence in awakening certain hidden faculties of the inner nature of man. They are necessarily very different from the conceptions of the waking state, which are, of course, for another kind of purpose—that of representing external objects. But the conceptions which the soul is to consider, when its object is the pursuit of spiritual training, are different. They are not for external representation, but are rather for the purpose of acting upon the soul—they are rather of emblematic, or symbolic presentment.

You must be able to shut out all other kinds of conception except the one. Ordinarily, the soul is divided among many conceptions at the same time. The important point of spiritual training is to be able to concentrate all your inner forces on one conception. This conception must be brought to the center of consciousness. Symbolic conceptions are more valuable than those which reflect outer objects or events, because the latter are of the outer world, and the soul has to depend less on itself than in the case of symbolic conceptions, as they are formed out of their own inner self. The first thing to be learned is the necessity of the intensity of the force to be exercised by the soul. It does not depend so much on what is before the soul, as the effort put forward, and the length of time concentrated on the conception. The longer time you concentrate on one subject, the more knowledge you stir up from the unknown depths of your soul.

The important object that should be in view

is the development of the right manner of concentration. This is accomplished by drawing away from the outer world at certain times, devoting your time to meditation. You gain by this a certain inner absorption of the symbolical conceptions. It is well to start the meditation by something you have seen and call to memory. Or you can look at a tree, then shut your eyes, and you can still see the image of the tree—almost as real as if you were still looking at it. Now this image or conception of the tree which you still have when not looking at it, we call a recollection. You then use this recollection to think of it. Shut everything out of your soul excepting the tree. The soul then dwells on the image of the tree. This is, of course, a perception that is actually seen by the senses, and for this very reason the necessary impulse is given for the awakening of the faculties of the soul. If, however, you proceed in the same way, but instead of choosing one of those conceptions which have already been tested by Seership, you choose some other, you can, in time, secure the same result.

At the present time, only one example will be given for meditation based on symbolical conception. You must build up this conception in your soul, as follows: Think of the growth of a plant from the time the seed is planted. First, the seed is planted, this sprouts and the plant appears. The roots spread in the ground; leaves shoot forth; and, finally, buds come, and the blossom, too, unfolds. Now think of a human being standing beside the plant and compare the human being with the plant and you will find that he has qualities and characteristics which are more perfect. The human being is able to move around wherever desired, while the plant cannot.

This shows that man has arisen to a higher stage of perfection than the plant, but there are qualities in man which the plant is devoid of, but which, as can be proven, make the plant more perfect than the man. Man, we know, is full of passions and desires, and these control his actions. By these a man commits many errors, but the plant is not so unfortunate. The law of its growth has passed on from leaf to leaf, and the passionless blossom opens its petals to the pure rays of the sun. On the other hand you say: "Man is possessed of certain faculties which exceed those of the plant, but he has attained these at the cost of allowing his impulses, passions and desires to commingle in his being with the purer forces recognized in the plant." Then we think of the green sap flowing through the plant, and think of it as the expressions of the pure and passionless law of growth. Contrast this with the blood running through the veins of man, and recognize this as expressive of man's instinct, of his passions and desires, and construct from all these a powerful thought within the soul. When we think of man's capacity for development, think how his instincts, passions, and desires may be purged and cleaned by the higher faculties of soul; then we must meditate on how the qualities are to be driven out, or transmuted to a higher plane, so that the blood may be finally called to mind as the expression of passion and desire, cleansed and purified.

Now think of a rose, saying to yourself: "In the red juice of the rose is the erstwhile green sap of the plant—now changed to crimson—and the red rose follows the same pure, passionless laws of growth as does the green leaf." Thus you may use the red rose as a symbol of a kind of blood which is the expression of cleansed impulses and passions, purified of all the lower elements, and which we can compare with the forces working in the red rose. This fact you must thoroughly understand. Think of the bliss, the purity and passionless nature of the plant, while man, to secure certain higher perception, had to have passions and desires. This you can ponder on, as it is worthy of serious consideration; while in its wake a sensation of liberating feeling may stir in you when you think of the red blood that can thus become the means of inward and pure experiences, as in the case of the red blood and the rose. You should not enter upon the line of thought necessary for the construction of such symbols, without feeling being present; after you have given the subject thought, and the feelings pursued, they should be transformed into the following symbolical conception: Think of a black cross standing before you, and let this mean the symbol of man's annihilated lower passions and desires, and then, where the beams of the cross traverse each other, think of this as seven bright red roses, ranged in a circle. Let the roses represent the symbol of that blood which is the expression of the cleansed and purified passions and desires.

You are now to call up before the soul this symbolical conception, as illustrated by the memory-conception. This, when contemplated on, has awakening power, if every other idea excepting this is excluded. See this symbol float before your soul, and just as plainly as possible.

The object in selecting the plant for an example was to show the nature of the plan and of man. The effect of analyzing the plant is to show how it is put together before it is used as a means for concentration. If you had just taken the plant, without analyzing its construction, you would not have been able to picture it in the mind so visibly. While meditating, the thoughts which come to you concerning the plant should not come from the soul. Think only of the image—imagine it is alive and floating through the air. Thus the plant becomes a sign, associated with an inner experience. The soul, by dwelling on the experience, produces the desired effect. The greater length of time you can concentrate on the symbol, without the conception arising to impose a disturbing element, the stronger will be the effect of the entire process. It is a good practice to use different things as a symbol. First study as a whole, then construct it as individual parts. Then see only as a whole floating through space, without letting anything disturb your vision.

HOW TO ATTAIN KNOWLEDGE OF THE HIGHER WORLDS

In every man there are latent faculties which, when developed, will enable him to gain knowledge of the higher worlds. To the seer, the soul world and the spirit world are just as real as the world we see with our physical eyes. What he has learned, you can learn when you have developed certain powers which today are slumbering within you. As long as the human race has existed there have always been some that have possessed these higher faculties, so we are not claiming that these are new powers; on the contrary, they have always existed. The knowledge has not been withheld from those who are ready for it. But, on the other hand, owing to its nature, it has always been kept a secret, and it is capable of doing great harm as well as good. Only those who have to a certain degree experienced these higher teachings can understand them.

Seership is a knowledge like any other; it is no more of a secret for the average man than writing is a secret to the savage. We know we can learn to write with the proper training; so can anyone develop Seership. In only one way are the two activities different. On the material plane of life it is necessary to have a certain amount of money to pay for the necessary training, but it requires no money to attain knowledge of the higher worlds. There is no obstacle in the way for the one who searches.

It is erroneously believed that it is necessary

to study under a teacher—one of the masters of the higher knowledge—before receiving any great enlightenment. However, any one who is earnest needs no teacher to lead him into the profound secrets of the world. There is always some one waiting to help you, if you are in earnest to attain the higher knowledge. There is a strict law to withhold from no one knowledge for which he is ready, but there is also a law that will not allow you to receive knowledge until you are ready for it. The more thoroughly you understand these two laws, the quicker your advancement will be.

The way in which Seership is developed, I have clearly described. Within the soul lies the power to become a seer. You must develop within yourself special faculties, and then the greatest treasures of the spirit become your own. It will be necessary to start with certain fundamental attitudes of the soul; only those who do can become seers.

The attitude of the mind of the Seer has much to do with his development, but you must not depend on faith for results; though, of course, you must believe that you can do something before you will be able to do it well. If a child was taught from the beginning (which will be done some day) that he can sense or feel coming events, or see distant places, and was encouraged and trained to do this, he would then acquire the power of Seership just as surely and as readily as he acquires the alphabet. Just as you learn to read your letters, you can learn to look into the future.

The science of Seership is like any other science. Some will be able to develop their psychic senses quicker and better than others, but all can develop them to a certain extent.

One of the most common errors I wish to correct here, and that is, that it is a gift with which some are born, and some not. It is a gift, to be true, and you are born with it because all are born with it. There is no monopoly on development; what I can do, you can do. All men will eventually develop the higher faculties. You will acquire them in time, or you may acquire them now, and be one of the extraordinary people.

I do not ask anyone to believe any statement in this book until it has been verified by him, which can be done if he takes the time. All I ask you to do is to start with an open mind. Follow me carefully, step by step; learn each phase carefully as you proceed. As your new powers develop, understand them thoroughly so you will not abuse them and suffer the consequences.

Do you like to read of great men? If you do, you have the making of a seer. This is the manifestation in you of the germ of Seership. It is a blessing when you begin to feel it. When you no longer desire to criticise; when you can see good in others; when you can hold your head erect, having purified yourself; when you can see your short-comings; then you are ready to become a seer and hear audible angel voices.

A WARNING

Do not crave for information concerning earthly

things. The higher faculties of the soul are to be used to gain knowledge of the spirit world and the general plan of the universe. The wise and exalted angels will not commune with you about material things.

There are many ready to attain marvelous development, if they would but train themselves. Remember, a strict integrity to one's highest light is essential to development. Self-abrogation and purity should be the aim of every one capable of communicating with the higher worlds.

If we do not develop within ourselves the knowledge that there is something within us higher than ourselves, we shall never realize that there is something higher. The seer acquires the power of leading his intellect to the heights of knowledge by guiding his heart into the depths of veneration and devotion. The heights of the spirit are reached by passing through the portals of humility. You acquire right knowledge when you learn to esteem it. You have the right gaze on reality, but you must first show by your actions that you are entitled to the right. There are certain laws of the spiritual as well as the physical world. If you rub a glass rod with the appropriate material it will become electric, and it will possess the power of attracting small bodies. This shows how natural law works. Every feeling of true devotion which comes from the soul, develops a power which may, sooner or later, lead to the development of Seership. This is one of the laws.

It is necessary that you possess within you this feeling of devotion, before you can gain entrance to the higher knowledge. If you do not possess this, it will be necessary for you to acquire it, which can be done by vigorous self-education, which will create the devotional mood within you. Full importance should be given to this. In the present state of civilization we are only too ready to criticise, expressing our opinions, and so forth, rather than having devotion and selfless veneration. Even children criticise far more than they worship. Every judgment, every sharp criticism frustrates the powers of the soul for the attainment of the higher knowledge, and in the same way all heart-felt devotion develops it. He who wishes to gain the higher development must create it within himself; he himself must instill it in his soul. He who wishes to become a seer must assiduously cultivate the devotional mood. He must look for that which demands of him admiration and homage. Whenever his duties permit, he should not criticise or pass judgment. If you look down on a man because he is weak, you rob yourself of the power to gain higher knowledge; but if you try to enter lovingly into his spirits, you then gather much power. Train yourself along these lines. It is necessary for you to learn to search for the good in all things, and to withhold of all carping criticism. Not only must this be your external action, but also your innermost action of the soul. Become a perfect being, and transform yourself completely, but this transformation must take place in your innermost self, in the mental life. It is not sufficient that you express your outward bearing towards a person;

you must also have this respect in your soul. Before you can become a seer it will be necessary for you to banish from your consciousness all thought of disrespect and criticism, and to cultivate thoughts of devotion.

Everything you do which helps you to banish from your consciousness whatever has remained of disparaging, suspicious judgment of your fellow-men, brings you nearer to becoming a seer. When once you fill your consciousness with thoughts which evoke in you admiration, respect and veneration for everything, you rise rapidly in your development. Those who have gone through this stage know that in these moments powers are awakened which otherwise would remain dormant. This is the way the spiritual eyes are opened. You begin to see new and interesting things around you, and realize that heretofore you have only seen a small part of the world around you. Your fellow-man now appears in quite a different aspect from what he has before. You will not at the time be able to see the human aura, as a still higher training is necessary for this, but you can reach this training after going through a thorough training in devotion.

The Seer does not appear any different than any ordinary person. You may live in close friendship with him, yet he will not impart any knowledge, because he knows you are not ready to receive it. He will only impart to you his secret when you are ready for it. Nothing will make him divulge to you anything which he knows should not be disclosed. Thus he goes on, noiseless and unnoticed by the outer world. There is no reason why any one should notice any particular difference in a seer. His duties he attends to as before, his appearance is the same as ever, it is only his inner part of the soul that is transformed, which is hidden from outward sight. In the beginning of the change the entire soul-life of man feels the devotion for everything venerable.

Those who are inexperienced will find it difficult to believe that feelings like reverence, respect and so forth, have anything to do with their perception. This is because you imagine that perception is a faculty within itself, and stands in no relation to what otherwise concerns the soul, but, remember, it is the soul that perceives. Your feelings affect the soul, like your food the body. If you should feed the body on crushed stone, your activity would soon cease. The same is true of the soul. It needs homage, veneration, devotion, which are the instruments that make it healthy and strong, and especially strong for the action of perception, while, on the other hand, antipathy, disrespect and under-estimation cause the starvation and withering of its activity. The seer can see all these in the aura. The soul which harbors the feelings of devotion and reverence brings a change in the aura. In the same way does the shape of your head change under different mental development. The phrenologist can read your character like an open book, by examining your head. As your feelings change, so does the color of your aura. In the person with feeling of devotion and reverence the aura will change from a certain yellowish, red or brown-red tint to tints of bluish-red. At this time the organ of perception opens. It is now ready to receive information of which heretofore it has had no knowledge. Reverence awakens a sympathetic power in the soul, and through this we attract similar qualities in others around us. Our power will become more effective with others' help. Gradually you learn to give yourself less to the impressions of the outer world, and, in its place, develop a vivid inward life. It will be useless for anyone to try to develop Seership if he changes from one impression of the outer world to another; if his entire thoughts are on dissipations. On the other hand, the seer must not shut himself out of the outer world. Once the inner life is realized, it will point out the direction in which he ought to lead his impressions. The man with a depth of soul and richness of emotion feels different from the man with few emotions. What we can experience within ourselves is what opens up the beauties of the outer world. One man may sail across an ocean, and only a few inward experiences may pass through his soul; while another may hear the eternal language of the world-spirit, and for him are unveiled the mysteries of creation.

To acquire intimate knowledge of even the outer world you must learn to control your feelings and ideas. All phenomenon of the outer world is full of divine splendor, but you must discover the divine within you before you can hope to discover it without. To become a seer you must set apart a part of the day during which time to withdraw from the outer world and be entirely alone. You should not think of your personal affairs, as this would bring about a result contrary to that wished for. Remain perfectly still, listen to the echoes of what you have experienced in the outer world. Secrets undreamed of will be revealed to you, and you will put yourself in the position to receive new impressions of the external world, as if you were looking upon it with different eyes. Those whose sole ambition is to enjoy impression after impression, stultify the perceptive faculty, while those who let the enjoyment afterwards reveal something to them, enlarge and educate it.

The disciple must necessarily pass through a host of temptations the purpose of each of which is to test the ego and to imprison it within itself. It should be wide open for the whole world. It is quite necessary that you should seek enjoyment, for in this way only can you prove that you are above temptation. If you mingle with the outer world and withstand their temptations, you are the better for it. If you are afraid of doing this, then it proves you fear the temptation. If you stop at the enjoyment, you will be the gainer by the contact with the outer world. While you live in this world, you should be of it, not dead to it. The seer considers enjoyment only as a means of ennobling himself to the world. He does not acquire great learning for himself alone, but that he may be of service to the world.

There is one important law which must never be transgressed, which is as follows: "Every branch of knowledge which you seek only to enrich your own learning, only to accumulate treasure for yourself, leads you away from the path; but all knowledge which you seek for working in the service of humanity and for the uplighting of the world, brings you forward." This law must always be lived up to. No one will be a seer until adopting it as a guide for his whole life.

Every idea which does not become an ideal for you, slays a power in your soul; every idea which becomes an idea, creates within you living powers.

I will now give you some practical directions which have been thoroughly tried by great teachers of the ancient and modern times.

Never let any one tamper with your individual independence. Seership teaches that you should respect and cherish human individuality. Keep watch over each of your actions, and each of your words, in order that you may not hinder the free-will of any human being. There is no need for any one to ·sacrifice his independence, in order to become a seer.

RULES TO BE REMEMBERED

Provide for yourself a place where you will not be disturbed. Sit in a comfortable position, and put yourself in a state of inward calm. Learn to distinguish between the real and unreal. The path is simple to follow, but only those will make a success who go about reaching the goal in an earnest way.

Set apart a certain time each day, if possible, to occupy yourself with something that is very different from your ordinary occupation. You will have to conduct yourself in a different way from the way you perform most of your duties. This does not mean that what you do will have no bearing on your general daily work; on the contrary, you will find that these few moments will enable you to do your daily work far better. The time depends on the amount of time at your disposal. You should give at least five minutes to it, which will be enough to start with, if necessary. The real point is the use you make of the time. Of course, the greater length of time you can meditate uninterrupted, the stronger will be the effect called forth. However, there is some danger of excess, as in everything else. After a little practice you will become conscious of a certain inward "marking of time," and this will advise you how long you should meditate.

During this time you should raise yourself above the work-day existence. Your thoughts and feelings should take on different coloring. Your joys and sorrows, cares, experiences, and actions must pass in review of the soul. You must cultivate a frame of mind which will enable you to regard all your experiences from a higher point of view. You should live your own life from the same high point of view you have regarding that of others. This is very necessary, as you are closely interwoven with your experiences and actions, while you only contemplate those of others. In these moments of meditation judge yourself as if you were some one else. Be a severe critic; when you do this, your own experiences will appear quite different. It is then you are able to separate the real from the unreal. The value of this contemplation does not depend so much on what you contemplate, as on the power which such inward calm develops.

In every one there is a higher consciousness than the one used in ordinary life. This higher being remains concealed until discovered. No one can awaken it for you; you must do it yourself. Just so long as this higher being is not aroused, the higher faculties of Seership will remain hidden. The inward calm opens up certain magic forces which set these free. Until these magic forces are felt within you, the rule mentioned should be followed. Every one who will carry out these instructions carefully will, in time, develop the spiritual sight, and then, a new world, and an existence you never dreamed of will be revealed to you.

As said before, there is no reason why there should be any outward change in your life. Your duties should be performed as before. In no manner should you estrange yourself from life. You should really be able to devote yourself more to it, because you do not waste so much time on things of no consequence. The few minutes of glimpses of the higher life will do you a lot of good. They will gradually have a remarkable influence on your ordinary life. Gradually you will grow calmer, and have serenity in all your actions, and will not become disturbed over mere trifles. The farther along the path you go, the less will circumstances and internal influences affect you. You will soon realize the wonderful advantage of these moments of contemplation. Things which formerly worried you, will cease to do so; things you used to fret over, will seem of little importance to you. You will lose all timidity, and the fear that you cannot do certain things you should do, but rather will say that you can do what you undertake to do. The new thought suppresses timidity.

This is the end of this publication.

Any remaining blank pages are for our book binding
requirements and are blank on purpose.

To search thousands of interesting publications like this one,
please remember to visit our website at:

http://www.kessinger.net

CPSIA information can be obtained
at www.ICGtesting.com
Printed in the USA
BVHW012244051122
651178BV00013B/249